# 6 Keys To
# Christian Growth

*How to live a victorious
Christian life*

Mark Weimer

**LCX**

LIFE CONNEXIONS
PEACHTREE CITY, GA

6 Keys to Christian Growth

Published by Life ConneXions
The Publishing Group of Campus Crusade for Christ
375 Highway 74 South, Suite A
Peachtree City, GA 30269
To order: (800) 827-2788

All Scripture quotations, unless otherwise indicated, are taken
from the Holy Bible: New International Version, © 1973,
1978, 1984 by the International Bible Society. Published by
Zondervan Bible Publishers, Grand Rapids, Michigan.

Cover photo: © David R. Stoecklin

Printed in the United States of America

ISBN: 1-56399-276-0

# Table of Contents

# Introduction

This book has been written to help you grow as a Christian. Once you have accepted Jesus Christ as your Savior, God wants you to live a victorious Christian life. The keys to this are simple — yet they can transform your life.

- You can be sure that you are God's child.
- You can be filled with God's power.
- You can know God's word.
- You can be part of God's people.
- You can experience God's presence.
- You can help carry out God's plan.

Jesus said, "I have come that they may have life, and have it to the full." May God bless you as you read this book — and as you apply each key in your life.

## KEY 1

# Be Sure You Are A Christian

Several years ago, I went to lunch with a couple I knew. At lunch, the husband said that he considered himself to be a Christian. His wife asked me what being a Christian was. I said that a Christian was someone who believed in God and had accepted Jesus Christ as their personal Savior.

The wife then turned to her husband and said "Well then, according to this, you're not a Christian are you?" The husband had thought that being a Christian meant agreeing with Christian principles like being kind to others. Somewhat taken aback, he now realized that might not be enough, since he really didn't believe in God or in Jesus Christ as his Savior.

What is a real Christian? The Apostle John in the Bible said "Yet to all who received Him, to those who believed in His name, He gave the right to become children of God."[1] How about you? As you're reading this book, are you sure that you're a Christian?

A couple of years ago, my wife and I were in the country of Sweden, visiting her grandparents' homeland. In talking to a very pleasant waitress, we asked if she was a Christian, and she said "Yes." As we talked some more, it became apparent that she didn't really believe in God or in Jesus Christ as her Savior, and didn't attend church; she simply felt that since she was born in Sweden, which is officially a Christian country, that that made her a Christian.

So what does it mean to be a Christian? The Bible states "For God so loved the world that He gave His one and only Son, that whoever believes in Him shall not perish but have eternal life."[2] The Apostle Paul said in Romans 10:9 "That if you confess with your mouth 'Jesus is Lord,' and believe in your heart that God raised Him from the dead, you will be saved."[3] To be a Christian you must believe in God and accept Jesus Christ as your Lord and Savior.

In order to distinguish between truth and falsehood, it is sometimes best to study the truth so we can see what is false more clearly. The United States Treasury Department has the job of identifying counterfeit money in the United States. One of the ways I have heard they train people to spot true versus counterfeit bills is not to study counterfeit bills, but to study real bills. If someone spends a long period of time studying a real twenty dollar bill, then when they see a counterfeit, they are much better able to spot it.

So it is with being a true Christian; we should study what is true. In order to help you figure out what being a Christian really is, the Bible makes it very simple. "If you confess with your mouth 'Jesus is Lord,' and believe in your heart that God raised Him from the dead, you will be saved."[4] This is a simple statement. Not *may* be saved, not *perhaps* will be saved, but *will* be saved. "This is the testimony: God has given us eternal life, and this life is in His Son."[5]

So who is God? He is the creator of the universe; the Bible says "In the beginning God created the heavens and the earth."[6] He is a spiritual being and is invisible; just as you cannot see the wind, so you cannot see God. God's nature is also loving and kind.

Picture the kindest, most loving person you know. Picture that person lovingly caring for a sick child. Multiply that love by a million and you catch a glimpse of the love of God. The Bible says "God is love."[7]

God is also all knowing and all wise. He knows what is best for us. I remember when I was teaching one of my children to ride a bike; I knew when to hold on to the bike and when it was safe to let go. In the same way, God knows how best to take care of us in wisdom and love.

God is perfectly moral and good in all He does. As earthly parents, we can sometimes be mad, or selfish, or act in wrong ways. But God in heaven is always good.

Jesus Christ is God's Son — God who came to earth and became a man. About 2,000 years ago Jesus was born in Bethlehem, in the country of Israel. God was His father, and His mother was a virgin named Mary. Jesus grew up to be a man and began His ministry when He was about 30 years old.

For the next 3 years He healed the sick; taught people about God; showed people the love of God; and did many miracles. He was put to death on a cross; even though He was perfect, He took the punishment that all of us deserved. The Bible says "He was pierced for our transgressions, He was crushed for our iniquities; the punishment that brought us peace was upon Him, and by His wounds we are healed. We all, like sheep, have gone astray, each of us has turned to his own way; and the Lord has laid on Him the iniquity of us all."[8]

Three days after His death He rose from the dead and appeared to His disciples. Then He rose into heaven, where He now sits at God's right hand. Someday Jesus will come again to reign as King of Kings and Lord of Lords.

Today here on earth, our key decision is whether we believe in Jesus. When some people came to Jesus here on earth, "They asked Him 'What must we do to do the works God requires?' Jesus answered: 'The work of God is this: to believe in the One He has sent.'"[9] Unlike the girl in Sweden who thought she was Christian just because she was born in a Christian country, we do not become a Christian just by where we were born. If you were born in a hospital, that does not make you a doctor or a nurse. If you were born in a barn, that does not make you a cow. Even though some countries may be labeled on the map "Christian countries," just being born there does not make you a Christian.

What about going to church? Going to church is a very good thing, but just attending church does not make you a Christian. If a mouse goes faithfully to a cookie jar once a week to eat cookies and spends an hour in that cookie jar once a week, that mouse does not become a cookie; he is still a mouse. He is a mouse, even though everything else in the cookie jar may be a cookie. If you go to church once a week faithfully, and many other people who are there are Christians, that still does not make you a Christian if you have not accepted Jesus Christ as your Savior.

What about good behavior? Some people think that if you simply do more good things than bad things, that makes you a Christian. This is also a false assumption. The Bible says "All have sinned and fall short of the glory of God."[10] It also says "There is no one righteous, not even one." [11] God is perfect and holy, and if we want to enter into eternal life on our own merits, we also must be perfect and holy. However, all of us — you and I, our families, and our friends — have all done or thought many things that are wrong. Imagine a contest to see who can swim to Hawaii from California, a distance of over 1,000 miles. A very bad swimmer might only make it a few hundred yards offshore before he cries for help. A great swimmer might make it three miles before he cries for help. However, no one will make it on their own effort.

So, if you can't trust in where you were born; if you can't trust in just doing good deeds; if you can't trust in just going to church; how can you know for sure that you are a Christian? Here are four simple steps that can help you know for sure if you are a Christian.

1. Realize that *God loves you and has a wonderful plan for your life.* Jesus said "I have come that they may have life, and have it to the full."[12] God loves you and wants you to know Him personally.

2. *We are sinful and separated from God,* and our own sins keep us from knowing God's love and plan for our life. The Bible says "For the wages of sin is death, but the gift of God is eternal life in Christ Jesus our Lord."[13] So our own attitudes and actions have created a gap between us and God. The key question is, how do we bridge this gap?

3. *Jesus Christ is God's only solution for man's sin.* Through Him, you can know and experience God's love and plan for your life.

Christ died in our place; He was buried and He rose from the dead. The Bible says "But God demonstrates His own love for us in this: While we were still sinners, Christ died for us."[14] "…The gift of God is eternal life in Christ Jesus our Lord."[15] It's not enough to know these three principles; we must individually receive Jesus Christ as our Savior and Lord.

4. *We must personally receive Christ.* "Yet to all who received Him, to those who believed in His name, He gave the right to become children of God."[16] We receive Christ through personal invitation. If you've never asked Christ into your life, you can do that by prayer right now. Prayer is talking to God. Here is a sample prayer that you could pray to ask Jesus Christ into your life:

*"Lord Jesus, I am sorry for my sins. Thank You for dying on the cross for me. I receive You as my Savior and Lord. Thank You for forgiving me and giving me the gift of eternal life. Take control of my life. Please make me the kind of person You want me to be."*

If this prayer expresses the desire of your heart, I invite you to pray this prayer right now, and Christ will come into your life, as He promised.

Whether you just prayed this prayer right now, or prayed a prayer like it many years ago, if you were sincere, Christ has come into your life as your Savior and Lord. How can you know this for sure? It's on the authority of God's word, the Bible. The Bible says "This is the testimony: God has given us eternal life, and this life is in His Son. He who has the Son has life; he who does not have the Son of God does not have life."[17]

In some ways it is like being married. When you take the vow to be married, you are legally married in the eyes of the church and of the state. Let's say one morning you wake up, and you are just so happy; you're madly in love and on top of the world — you are still married. Let's say a week later, you've just had a fight with your spouse and are feeling upset — you are still married. You're just as married when you're happy as when you're mad; legally there is no difference.

In much the same way, you are a Christian because you've been born again through your faith in Jesus Christ. If you wake up one morning, and feel very close to God and very spiritual, that is great, but your feelings don't make you a Christian. You are a Christian because you have accepted Christ. If you wake up the next morning and feel depressed and far away from God, you are still a Christian because you have accepted Christ.

You can thank God every day that Christ is in your life as your Savior and Lord. Because of Christ in your life and your faith in Him, you have the gift of eternal life and you are a child of God. You can be sure that you are a Christian.

Think of your relationship with God as being part of a family. Now that you are a Christian, you can live as part of that family. If you sin, you can ask God to forgive you. The Bible says "If we confess our sins, He is faithful and just and will forgive us our sins and purify us from all unrighteousness."[18]

You have probably experienced in your own life times when you have argued with someone and felt a real distance between the two of you. You don't have to let this happen between you and God. If you have sinned or fallen away or done something that makes you feel distant from God, you can come back to Him. He loves to hear from you. As a Christian, you can sincerely ask His forgiveness, in Jesus' name, and He will forgive you. This is a key part of keeping your relationship with God strong and healthy — don't let unconfessed sin pile up in your life. You can grow every day in your relationship with God just as a loving child and loving father grow in their relationship together.

If you have accepted Jesus Christ as your Savior and Lord, you can be sure you are a Christian. This is the first key to Christian growth.

# KEY 2

# Be Filled with the Holy Spirit

Picture a fire fighter heading into a building that is ablaze with fire. The fire is devouring the entire first floor, and the fire fighter is ready. He has his uniform on; his protective helmet and his ax are ready. He grabs the hose connected to the water supply and charges the fire. As he nears the flames, he turns on the hose, ready to conquer the fire; only to find, to his surprise, that the water supply is turned off and he is helpless against the great blaze.

That is exactly how a Christian is trying to combat sin or evil without the power of the Holy Spirit. As Christians we can think we are all equipped and prepared, but without the Holy Spirit in our lives, we are overmatched by the fire. You need the Holy Spirit to effectively live the Christian life. Jesus said "You will receive power when the Holy Spirit comes on you;

and you will be My witnesses in Jerusalem, and in all Judea and Samaria, and to the ends of the earth."[1]

Who is the Holy Spirit? Quite simply, the Holy Spirit is God Himself, here on earth, in a spiritual, invisible form. Think of a little boy, looking out the window at clothes hanging on the line, blowing in the breeze.

"Mom," he asks, "why are those clothes flapping like that?"

"Well, Billy," the mother replies, "the wind is blowing them."

"But, mom," said Billy, "I can't see the wind. How can something invisible make our clothes move?"

The Holy Spirit is much like that. A man named Nicodemus came to Jesus and said "'Rabbi, we know You are a teacher who has come from God. For no one could perform the miraculous signs You are doing if God were not with him.'

In reply Jesus declared, 'I tell you the truth, no one can see the kingdom of God unless he is born again.'

'How can a man be born when he is old?' Nicodemus asked. 'Surely he cannot enter a second time into his mother's womb to be born!'

Jesus answered 'I tell you the truth, no one can enter the kingdom of God unless he is born of water and the Spirit. Flesh gives birth to flesh, but the Spirit gives birth to spirit. You should not be surprised at My saying, "You must be born again." The wind blows wherever it pleases. You hear its sound, but you cannot tell where it comes from or where it is going. So it is with everyone born of the Spirit.'[2]

You hear the sound of wind through the trees, but you don't know where it goes. So it is with everyone born of the Holy Spirit. The key is to seek the invisible power of God moving in your life.

Picture a dry sponge being put into a tub of water. As the water fills the sponge, soon it is filled to overflowing with water. When you take the sponge out of the water, water just flows out of the sponge.

This same concept is much like what is described when the Bible talks about being baptized in the Holy Spirit. Jesus said to His disciples "Do not leave Jerusalem, but wait for the gift My Father promised, which you have heard Me speak about. For John baptized with water, but in a few days you will be baptized with the Holy Spirit."[3] A number of days later, the disciples were praying, and on the day of the Jewish feast of Pentecost "All of them were filled with the Holy Spirit..."[4] How can we be filled with the Holy Spirit? When we accept Jesus Christ as our Savior and Lord, we have the privilege of being filled with the Holy Spirit of God.

Is being filled with the Holy Spirit a one time event or is it something that happens on a continual basis? The answer is that both statements are true. When you build a house, the house is dark with no lights until you hook up electricity. You put wiring in the house one time and the house then has electricity; however, you also turn on the electricity every time you enter a room or every time that you need light. We receive the Holy Spirit initially, spiritually, by faith. We then choose, on an ongoing basis, to be filled with the Holy Spirit.

The Apostle Paul said in his letter to the Ephesians, "Be filled with the Spirit."[5] The verb tense in original Greek would actually be better translated "be continually being filled with the Holy Spirit." The Bible describes a continual action, one that we would do on an ongoing basis. For example, if you said to someone they should breathe, what you are really meaning is that they should breathe on a continual basis, not just one time. So it is with the

Holy Spirit; we should seek to be continually filled with the Holy Spirit.

How do we know if we are filled with the Holy Spirit? We can know that we are filled with the Holy Spirit by faith, on the authority of God's word.

If you are a citizen of a particular country, say the United States of America, you are made a citizen one time; you continue to be a citizen every day after that. You can wake up every morning with the confidence that you are a citizen of the United States. You may feel very pro-American one day, and you may not feel so American the next. In any case, you are a citizen every day from that point on for the rest of your life.

If you ask God to fill you with His Holy Spirit, you can trust that God will give the Holy Spirit to those that ask Him. Jesus said "If you then, though you are evil, know how to give good gifts to your children, how much more will your Father in heaven give the Holy Spirit to those who ask Him."[6] God did not intend for you to have to live the Christian life in your own power, like a fire fighter battling a blaze with no water. God, the Holy Spirit, will come and live in your life and in your heart. You have the wonderful privilege of being filled with the Holy Spirit of God on a daily, ongoing basis.

If you are a Christian and have never asked to be filled with the Holy Spirit, you can do so right now. Here's a suggested prayer: "Dear God, thank You that You love me and thank You for sending Your son Jesus to die on the cross for my sins. Please fill me with Your Holy Spirit. I give You control of my life. Thank You for giving me the gift of the Holy Spirit. In Jesus' name, amen."

If you've already asked to be filled with the Holy Spirit, then thank God by faith that you are filled with the Holy Spirit. You can seek God on an ongoing basis, everyday, and ask Him to fill, control and empower you by the Holy Spirit. God has given you the gracious gift of His own presence in your life by the power of the Holy Spirit. You can thank God every day that He is in your life.

Realize that the gift of the Holy Spirit is not given to you just for special times when you really need God. God truly wants you to enjoy His presence at all times. You also have the ability to choose, each day, to walk controlled by the Holy Spirit. Picture walking into a darkened room. You can choose to wander around in the dark, or you can go to the light switch and flip on the light. Or picture taking out a boat which has both oars and a motor. If you want, you can row the boat yourself; however, a far better choice if you are trying to get some place quickly is to turn on the motor and let the motor give power to the boat.

The Christian life is much more than just a list of rules. If you try to live the Christian life alone, on your own strength, you will inevitably fail. People have tried and failed for many years. The Bible speaks of "Christ in you, the hope of glory."[7] Jesus said, "I am the vine; you are the branches. If a man remains in Me and I in him, he will bear much fruit; apart from Me you can do nothing."[8] The Holy Spirit is referred to as our "helper" in the Bible. As you walk and live your life controlled by the Holy Spirit, then God Himself will fill you and flow through you to touch others.

God has sent the Holy Spirit to fill you on a day by day basis. God Himself, in the person of the Holy Spirit, can live His life through you. God can give you power by the Holy Spirit to overcome evil desires. "So I say, live by the Spirit, and you will not gratify the desires of the sinful nature."[9]

The apostle Paul said "But the fruit of the Spirit is love, joy, peace, patience, kindness, goodness, faithfulness, gentleness and self-control."[10] Just as a plant bears fruit, so the Holy Spirit bears these fruits in our lives.

Are you having a hard time loving someone? Ask Jesus, by the Holy Spirit, to flow through your life. Jesus prayed for forgiveness for those people who were crucifying Him as He hung on the cross. He can provide the love for you to love those who have hurt you.

God can also lead and guide you by His Holy Spirit. "When the Counselor comes, whom I will send to you from the Father, the Spirit of truth who goes out from the Father, He will testify about Me."[11] Jesus said He would not leave us as orphans, but would leave the Holy Spirit to be with us. Are you having a hard time believing in God to overcome some obstacles in life? Rather than just trying to muster up confidence yourself, ask God, by the Holy Spirit, to give you faith and the wisdom to act on that faith. The Apostle Peter, when Jesus was about to be crucified, denied Jesus three times, driven by his fear. Only a few weeks later, when filled with the

Holy Spirit, he spoke boldly to thousands of people in Jerusalem about Christ.

You can ask God on a daily basis to fill you with His Holy Spirit. He can fill you with His Spirit and give you His love and joy. So the second key to Christian growth is to be filled with God's Holy Spirit each and every day.

# KEY 3

# Learn God's Word

Many men in America have a bad reputation — that we don't want to follow instructions. It is almost a joke that a man will drive around lost rather than stop to ask directions.

I remember a time when I was putting together a swing set for my children. The set looked very easy when it was fully assembled in the pictures, but when I took it out of the box at home, there were over 450 individual parts. What did I do? Even though I am an American man, I decided to grab the instruction manual because I knew I couldn't put the swing set together on my own and I wanted to make sure I put it together right.

God has given us an instruction manual, and that manual is the Bible. In Psalms 119, it says "Your word is a lamp to my feet and a light for my path."[1] God has given us the Bible as an instruction manual to help us learn how to live the Christian life and to know Him better. Before all else fails, read the manual. In other words, don't be like the typical American male and wait until you are totally lost to ask for directions.

In addition to giving us helpful instructions for life, the Bible is spiritually inspired and has supernatural power. When Jesus began His ministry, He spent forty days in the desert. During that time He was tempted by the devil. Even though Jesus was the Son of God and had all of the power in the universe at His disposal to use against Satan, the weapon that He chose to use was to quote scripture — the word of God. When He was tempted, Jesus replied "It is written, 'Man does not live on bread alone, but on every word that comes from the mouth of God.'"[2] If that kind of spiritual power was what Jesus chose to use, you and I can use that in our own lives as well.

In the Book of Ephesians, the apostle Paul talked about the spiritual armor that we as Christians can put on to help us to be victorious in our spiritual lives. "Finally, be strong in the Lord and in His mighty power. Put on the full armor of God…Take the helmet of salvation and the sword of the Spirit, which is the word of God."[3] The sword is the one offensive weapon listed; that sword, according to Paul, is the word of God.

Where did the Bible, the word of God, come from? The Bible is a collection of sixty six books written over a period of approximately 1,500 years by many different authors who were inspired by God. These books were collected and recognized by godly men of old as inspired by God.

Why should we study the Bible? In Paul's second letter to Timothy, he said "All scripture is God-breathed and is useful for teaching, rebuking, correcting and training in righteousness, so that the man of God may be fully equipped for every good work."[4] Paul was saying that scripture helps us in several ways.

One way is that we learn doctrine, the foundations of our faith; what it is that we should believe, and what is important in the Christian life. A second is that the Bible can give us instruction concerning specific moral issues. There may be areas in your or my life to which the Bible can speak. For me personally, a number of times I will read something from the Bible and it will be as if God says to me through that scripture, "This is for you." Once I was working at a job and had some problems with my boss. In several places the New Testament talks about servants honoring their masters, even if their masters are not godly. Through the Bible it was as if God spoke to me about my having an attitude in which I needed to honor my boss.

The Bible also helps train us in righteousness, so that we will recognize righteousness and apply it to our lives. One example of this is the Bible speaking about pride and humility. Picture a young man John, who has a speech to give the next day. He is very focused on how he looks, so that everyone will think he does a great job. The night before he gives this speech, he reads in the Bible "When pride comes, then comes disgrace, but with humility comes wisdom."[5] As a result, the next day, John decides to focus much more on God and on the people he's speaking to, as opposed to how he looks and what people think of him.

Paul also says the purpose of scripture is so that "...the man of God may be thoroughly equipped for every good work."[6] Through the Bible, God wants to build character into our lives. The goal is not just to know about good doctrine and what we should do, but through the Bible God works character qualities into our lives so that we will be prepared for good works. Don't just study the Bible to gain knowledge. God's goal is that you will take the principles in the Bible and as you apply them to your own life, you can then express those principles through good works and be a blessing to others.

The Bible is also very practical. One example of this is in the area of worship and praise. The Bible tells us who should praise God — "Let everything that has breath praise the Lord."[7] The Bible gives an example of how often to praise God — "Every day I will praise You."[8] It encourages us to sing and give thanks to God — "Let us come before Him with thanksgiving and extol Him with music and song."[9]

How is the Bible organized? The Bible is divided into two major sections, the Old Testament and the New Testament. The Old Testament covers the period of time from creation through the history of the Jewish people up until before the time of Jesus. The New Testament talks about the period of time from Jesus' birth to the beginning of the early church (about A.D. 1 to A.D. 60).

Depending on what you are looking for in the Bible, there may be different places you can search. For example, if you were looking for baseball advice and had a book available to you written by the greatest players who have ever played the game, you might go to one place to find out about how to throw the ball from the greatest pitcher of all time. If you wanted to learn how to hit the ball, you would go to a section written by the best hitters of all time. In the same way, there are different parts of the Bible where you can get advice on different areas of your life.

The first books in the Old Testament talk about history from the creation of the world and how the Jewish people would sometimes serve God and at other times fall away from God. This is followed by Psalms, a collection of 150 songs or poems. The Psalms are a great place to go to learn about worship and to learn how to react in a godly way to the joys and struggles of life. The Book of Proverbs contains 31 chapters full of practical advice about how to live your life. For example, you could read one chapter of Proverbs each day of the month and gain great wisdom. Later in the Old Testament come the Prophets, writings of godly prophets who spoke God's word to Israel; their messages can still apply to us today. "Your word, O Lord, is eternal; it stands firm in the heavens."[10]

The New Testament starts off with four books, Matthew, Mark, Luke and John, the history of

Jesus' life here on earth. This is followed by the book of Acts, the story of the early church. A series of letters follows, many of them written by the Apostle Paul. They are very helpful because they are letters to Christians, addressing issues of faith, doctrine and how to live the Christian life. The last book of the Bible is the Book of Revelation, which contains many prophecies about the future.

How should you read the Bible? How often should you study it? There are no specific rules here, but many Christians believe that it is an excellent habit to read the Bible every day. Picture a young girl named Helen starting a new diet. Her mom asks, "What would you like for dinner?" Helen says, "That's OK, Mom, I am only eating one day a week now, but I eat enough on that day for the whole week." Helen's mom would think she was crazy. Just as you would not go a day without taking in physical food that your body needs for nourishment, so by reading the Bible every day, you can receive spiritual food and insight from God.

The writer of Psalms said "Oh, how I love Your law! I meditate on it all day long."[11] A pastor I heard once encouraged people to read three chapters from their Bible each day; one from the Old Testament, one from the New Testament, and one from either Psalms or Proverbs. This is just one suggestion. There are many ways to study the Bible, but you will probably find it helpful to set a regular time to read the Bible every day.

Bear in mind that the purpose of reading the Bible is not to fulfill some religious obligation; it is your blueprint for living a godly, spiritually healthy life. In the U.S. there is an elite group of naval airplane pilots known as the Blue Angels. They entertain crowds by doing amazing stunts, rolling planes upside down, and performing fantastic flying feats. One Blue Angels pilot talked about learning to fly and being given two enormous manuals about his F-18 jet. He studied those manuals diligently so that he would be totally familiar with every important aspect of his plane and he would know best how to fly. In the same way, God has given us the Bible as His "instruction book" for living a Christian life. The Bible can help us understand even our own heart. "For the word of God is living and active. Sharper than any double-edged sword, it penetrates even to dividing soul and spirit, joints and marrow; it judges the thoughts and attitudes of the heart."[12]

Just as when eating physical food, it is helpful to have a well-balanced diet — to have vegetables, fruits, breads and protein — so when you read the Bible, it is helpful to have a balanced spiritual diet. As a new Christian, it is helpful to focus most of your reading on the New Testament, but you can then branch out to Psalms, Proverbs and parts of the Old Testament as well. Through reading the Bible, God can help strengthen you in your spiritual life. In Psalm 119, the Bible says "I have hidden Your word in my heart that I might not sin against You."[13] When God's word is implanted in your heart through study and prayer it can help to strengthen your faith.

You can also study the Bible in groups or with others. Your own personal study time is invaluable, but often you can learn through sitting under the teachings of a gifted Bible teacher and through small group discussions with others. My old pastor used to encourage us in his congregation not just to believe his teaching because he said it, but to check things out for ourselves in the Bible. This is a good guideline; respect and honor your pastor, but also read and study the Bible yourself.

A final thought to remember is that the purpose of reading the Bible is not just to learn information, but to see God apply it to your life. The book of Psalms says "How can a young man keep his way pure? By living according to Your word."[14]

A great jazz musician put it this way. He encouraged musicians to study their jazz skills and to practice diligently. Yet when it came time to stand up and play, musicians should realize that they wouldn't have time to think about how to play each song — the knowledge gained would already be in their lives. In other words, "just get up there and play." You should store up God's word in your heart so that it will be there when you need it.

Our goal is that God's word would be hid in our hearts and lives and would help give us the foundation to live a strong Christian life. "I trust in Your word."[15] In this way we can go out and be used of God to change the world for Jesus Christ. So the third key to Christian growth is to learn God's word.

# KEY 4

# Be Involved In Church

In the winter our family would often have fires in the fireplace. One thing I quickly discovered was that to have a fire of real wood which lasted for a while, you needed several logs burning together. With just one log, no matter how much you try to light it on fire, it doesn't stay lit for a long period of time.

This is similar to what happens when you become a Christian. God designed us as Christians in such a way that we need each other. When we meet together and help, encourage and learn from each other, we are like logs in the fireplace that burn together and provide a lasting fire. If we are separate and go our own way alone, that fire could quickly die down. That's one of the reasons the Bible says "Let us not give up meeting together, as some are in the habit of doing, but let us encourage one another..."[1] The application of this for you and me is that each of us, as Christians, needs to actively participate with other Christians in fellowshipping, in learning and in spending time together.

The early church met together continually. "They devoted themselves to the apostles' teaching and to the fellowship, to the breaking of bread and to prayer...All the believers were together and had everything in common...Every day they continued to meet together in the temple courts. They broke bread in their homes and ate together with glad and sincere hearts, praising God and enjoying the favor of all the people. And the Lord added to their number daily those who were being saved."[2]

As the church spread out from Israel, they would gather together and meet in new communities. Modern day Greece and Turkey were the earliest areas outside of Israel where the church met. Even when there were only a few believers, they would meet together for teaching, for fellowship, and to minister to one another and send missionaries into the world.

What is church? One problem we have in the English language is that the word "church" has come to mean a church building, and so it is easy to think of church as being the place where we go to have services on Sunday. If you think of large groups of people in the world, for example military forces, they do not generally define themselves by a particular location. The U.S. Army is a large group of people who are all over the world. They may move from place to place; they live in barracks or in tents and may meet in different places; but they are defined by being a group of people, not just a location.

Although the church is very different from the U.S. Army in its purpose and mission, it is similar in that it too is a group of people. The Apostle Paul said of Jesus "...He is the head of the body, the church."[3] So the church is really the body of Christ. Christ is on this earth, right now, through the person of the Holy Spirit — He is just invisible. When He was on earth, He inhabited one physical human body. Now that Christ is on earth through the Holy Spirit, you and I as individual Christians all together make up the body of Christ. "And God placed all things under His feet and appointed Him to be head over everything for the church, which is His body, the fullness of Him who fills everything in every way."[4] We are His hands and we are His feet. When Christ goes out to minister and to love, it will often be through us. A concept called the universal body of Christ refers to all of the Christians together in the whole world that have ever lived who make up the body of Christ.

Picture little Timmy and his two friends, Jeffery and Sandra, outside in the backyard. They are sitting on the grass, and little Timmy has his hands together as if he was praying. Timmy's mom comes outside and says "What are you doing, children?"

Sandra replies, "We are having church!"

The mom says, "Well, where is the church building and steeple?"

Timmy replies to this, "Mom, our church doesn't have much money. So we can't afford a steeple, but we are still having church!"

Sometimes little kids can be wiser than us adults. Timmy was right — while it is great to have nice buildings, what is most important is the presence of Jesus. Jesus said "For where two or three come together in My name, there am I with them."[5] What is important is that the church through the centuries has met together and prayed together under the leadership of the Holy Spirit, as the body of Christ.

Picture a young man John saying, "But I don't get much out of going to church."

To this, his friend Hal quickly replied, "That's not the only reason to go to church, to get something."

There are many reasons for us to go to church. One is to learn from the teachings of the pastor or the elder that God has appointed. You can ask God to speak to you through the teachings on a regular basis. It is also important to be baptized; Jesus said that we should be baptized in the name of the Father, and the Son, and the Holy Spirit.

Another reason to go to church is to participate and help others; not just to receive yourself, but to serve and to minister to others within your church. You can teach children, you can help minister to those who are sick or you can help in other ways. The Golden Rule is "So in everything, do to others what you would have them do to you."[6] There are many ways that you can serve God by ministering to others in the church. In the early church, there was a need for someone to care for widows and help those who did not have enough food. As a result, the apostles appointed a number of deacons to help in the day to day ministry to others.

Another important purpose of church is to worship God together, in song and in focusing on the Lord. There are many examples of the ancient Jewish people gathering together to worship and praise God in song. The Bible says "Praise our God, O peoples, let the sound of His praise be heard..."[7]

At church you can also join together with others in praying to God. When the apostle Peter was imprisoned in the early days of the church, "the church was earnestly praying to God for him."[8] God answered their prayers. Jesus said "I tell you that if two of you on earth agree about anything you ask for, it will be done for you by My Father in heaven."[9]

The late U.S. President, John F. Kennedy, said in his inaugural address "Ask not what your country can do for you, but ask what you can do for your country." That's a good balance for all of us. Don't ask just what your church can do for you, but what you can do for your church. How can you be an active participant, both receiving and also ministering to others in your local church?

The largest church in the world at the beginning of the 21st century was the Full Gospel Central Church of Seoul, Korea, with 800,000 members. In such a large church, it can be hard to get to know people in the Sunday church services. One of the things God uses to draw the church together is an enormous network of over 50,000 small groups. Every week, believers all over Seoul meet together in small groups. There they receive teaching, they pray for one another, they minister to one another and they discuss ways to reach out to their neighbors who are not Christians.

The Bible also gives us an example of believers meeting both in large and small groups, saying of the early church "Every day they continued to meet together in the temple courts. They broke bread in their homes and ate together."[10] There are some things that can happen easier in a small group than a large meeting. If you have a prayer request, a small group of people can pray for you and get to know you. Many churches around the world are actually house churches. The entire church may be a group of ten or twenty people meeting in a home or small meeting place. There's a warmth and richness of fellowship and care that can happen in a small house church like this or in a small group as part of a larger church.

If you are a Christian and are not part of a small group, I encourage you to ask God to give you a small group of people to meet with. You should still faithfully attend your large group meetings, but you can also grow as part of a small group. For example, on college campuses, there may be Christian groups that meet together. You can pray together, minister to one another, encourage one another and hold each other accountable in Christ's love. There is a scripture "As iron sharpens iron, so one man sharpens another."[11] We grow together as we lift each other up in love and accountability and encouragement. God can use other Christians to encourage you and help you grow as a Christian.

How does God lead you to a good church? Picture a couple, Nancy and Jim, moving to a new town and wanting to find a church. Nancy and Jim had recently accepted Christ as their Savior, and wanted to find a church where they could grow in their faith, as well as reach out and help others. They prayed and asked God to lead them to a good church. Shortly after they prayed, they met two of their neighbors who both attended a local community church just down the street from them. Then, one of the girls on their block, the same age as their own daughter, invited their daughter to come to her Sunday school class at the same church. They went to the church and discovered that it was a church that faithfully taught the Bible, and they felt God's love and warmth there. They prayed, sensed God's peace about their decision, and soon they were involved in that local church.

How do you find the church God wants you to attend? For many people in the world, the answer is unfortunately relatively easy, because there's only one church in their area. In the Book of Acts in the Bible, this was the case; a church was formed in a new city, and that was the entire group of believers. If this is the case, and it's a good church, you should go to that church.

For others of us, there may be different churches in the area in which you live. Two suggestions here would be to pray and to go. James said in the Bible "If any of you lacks wisdom, he should ask God, who gives generously to all without finding fault, and it will be given to him."[12] Pray that God will lead you to the right church, and then go and get involved and try churches where the Bible is preached. Here are some elements to look for in a church:

1) Do they preach from the Bible?
2) Do they believe that through faith in Christ alone, someone can be saved?
3) Do they recognize all true Christians as being part of the body of Christ?
4) Can you sense Christ's spirit and love in that congregation?

5) Is their vision and faith consistent with what you feel God is calling you to?

As you go to church, realize that the church won't be perfect; you will find imperfect people in that church (you may even be one yourself). Even the early church in the Bible was full of imperfect people, but they still met together and ministered to one another and worshipped Christ.

You can worship God, become a stronger Christian and minister to others in your local church. So the fourth key to Christian growth is to get involved in your local church.

# KEY 5

# Spend Time With God

Picture a little five year old girl, Amanda, standing outside in her backyard. She has some flowers in her hand, playing with the petals. Her dad comes outside and notices that it looks as though she's talking to herself.

"Are you talking to yourself, Amanda?" her dad asks.

"No, daddy," she says, "I'm talking to God. He's my friend, and He listens to me, and I listen to Him."

Amanda had the right idea. In the Bible, Jesus said "I tell you the truth, unless you change and become like little children, you will never enter the kingdom of heaven."[1] As adults, we sometimes want to make prayer very formal and organized. But the heart of prayer is just talking to God and spending time with Him. If you are a Christian, you can talk to God any time — He is with you wherever you go.

Going to church is an important time when we can pray. However, we should be aware we don't just meet with God when we go to church or at other special times — God is with us wherever we are. "God has said, 'Never will I leave you; never will I forsake you.'"[2] Jesus promised to send the Holy Spirit when He left this earth. Jesus said "And surely I am with you always, to the very end of the age."[3] You can know, as a Christian, that God is with you always, whether you're driving in the car, working in the garden, going to church or spending time with your family. God is with you wherever you are.

If God is with us always, then how should we pray? Imagine two friends, Stacy and Ann. Whenever Stacy calls Ann on the phone, she says things like "Ann, I really need help with some extra money this week because I'm running short." "Ann, I have a lot of problems I want to tell you about." "Ann, could you give me advice on this?" "Ann, could you come over and help me with my job this afternoon?"

If this just happened once in a while, if Ann is a good friend she would probably listen to Stacy and try to help her out as much as possible. But if every time they talk, Stacy spent the entire conversation asking Ann for help, don't you think Ann would think it was a little bit of a one-sided relationship? In much the same way, if our prayer times with God are always asking Him for things, and never stopping to listen or just enjoy spending time with Him, that is somewhat of a one-sided relationship.

Prayer should be talking with God; it is similar in some ways to how you would build an earthly relationship with someone. You would take time to listen; you would tell them things you appreciate about them; and you would ask for advice. In short, you would get to know them as a person during this special time. One of the aspects of prayer that is very important is to listen to God; to spend time in silence and to give Him time to speak to your heart so it is not a one-way conversation.

Is there a special pattern we should always use when we pray? When the disciples of Jesus asked Him to teach them to pray, He taught them the Lord's Prayer:

"Our Father in heaven, hallowed be Your name."[4] He taught them to honor God and to worship Him and give Him praise.

"Your kingdom come, Your will be done on earth as it is in heaven."[5] He taught His disciples to pray for God's will, to submit to God's will, and to ask that God's will would be done on earth as it is in heaven.

"Give us today our daily bread."[6] Here Jesus taught His followers to pray each day, to acknowledge their dependence on God, and to pray for their daily needs.

"Forgive us our debts, as we also have forgiven our debtors."[7] We acknowledge our forgiveness from God each day, and ask for forgiveness from Him if we have sinned against Him. We also commit to forgive others who have sinned against us.

"And lead us not into temptation, but deliver us from evil."[8] We are to ask God to keep us from temptation and to protect us from evil; we are very dependent on God for His help in resisting sin in our lives.

"For yours is the kingdom and the power and the glory forever."[9] We end by acknowledging our praise and worship of God; that the kingdom of the entire universe belongs to Him; that He is due all honor; and that all power truly and ultimately belongs to God.

Jesus Himself gave us His example of praying in different times and in different ways. An example of this flexibility could be like two different people who work for two different companies. One company has a 500 page manual that covers every exact situation. When you talk with the customer service representative from that company, you feel like you're talking to a machine, because all the person ever does is check with the manual and read you a response. The second company teaches its employees to take great care of customers and to work with them and understand their needs. When you talk to a person from the second company, you feel like you're talking to a real person who listens to you and works with you and responds to you and takes care of you.

It's much the same way in our communication with God. If we just recite prayers, saying the same prayers everyday as if reading from a manual, that may not be very high quality communication. If you talked to your child, and every day your child said exactly the same thing to you, reading their answers from a book, you would probably not feel like your child was really communicating with you. God wants to hear prayers from our hearts.

When should you pray? At one time "…Jesus told His disciples a parable to show them that they should always pray and not give up."[10] Jesus honors persistent prayer. Realize that at all times God is with you, and you can be praying to Him in your heart and your spirit at all times.

At the same time, it's good to spend uninterrupted time alone with God. Just as it is good to spend uninterrupted time with the people in your family, it is important to spend uninterrupted time with God. In the Bible, David said "In the morning, O Lord, You hear my voice; in the morning I lay my requests before You and wait in expectation."[11] The early morning is one possible time to spend uninterrupted time with God.

How much time should you spend? The Bible does not give us a specific amount of time to pray. However, think about it logically — if you wanted to build a relationship with the person who is the most important person in the world to you, do you think you could do this with one minute of uninterrupted time a day? I don't think so. Ask God to lead you and guide you in spending time with Him each day, and how much time would be good. In addition to uninterrupted time, as you go through the day, you can talk to God about your wants, your needs, your fears, your hopes and your dreams.

It is also important to take time praising and thanking God. He is the Lord of the universe and we need to give Him honor and praise. The Lord's Prayer begins and ends with praise and thanksgiving to God. When the Pilgrims came to America in the 1500's, their lives were very difficult. They had left their old homes in hope of a better life. The voyage across the Atlantic was very difficult. Their ship the Mayflower was not a boat like today's cruise liners where everything is well taken care of; an unknown future lay ahead of them.

Once they landed in America, it was near the current city of Boston. However, there was no beautiful city and airport to greet them, no hotels, no taxi drivers, and no warm rooms to settle into. They had to build their own houses and buildings and gather their own food, and a cold winter lay ahead. Yet, when they gathered in November of that first year, they specifically set up a time of thanksgiving to give thanks and praise to God for who He was and for what He had done. Their attitude was one of praise and thanksgiving to God for many blessings, even in the midst of times of testing and challenges.

Our lives can be like this as well. Sometimes we experience great blessings and joys, and other times we may endure great difficulties and hardships. Whether in good times or in bad, we have the joy and privilege of praising God; of thanking Him for who He is, and of praising Him for what He has done in our lives. Praise and thanksgiving are important parts of our relationship with God. "Enter His gates with thanksgiving and His courts with praise; give thanks to Him and praise His name."[12]

Jesus said the greatest commandment is "Love the Lord your God with all your heart and with all your soul and with all your mind and with all your strength. The second is this: 'Love your neighbor as yourself.'"[13] How can we love God? We often think of this in terms of doing things for God, and that clearly is one important way. At the same time, just as an earthly parent loves to hear the words "I love you" from his child, so God loves to hear the words "I love you" from us. You can tell God that you love Him, you can enjoy spending time with Him and you can even sing worship songs to God. God is not so concerned about whether you have a good singing voice or not; He looks at your heart. We are to "Praise Him for His acts of power; praise Him for His surpassing greatness."[14] Jesus said that true worshipers would worship God in spirit and in truth, and that God seeks those that worship Him in this way.

One of the great virtues of church is that it gives you a chance to express worship to God together. Don't just sing songs without thinking in church, but picture God in heaven receiving your love and adoration. Enjoy spending time with Him. In the Broadway musical, Fiddler on the Roof, the hero Tevye asks his wife if she loves him. At first she responds by saying "For 25 years I have washed your clothes," and points out all the various things she has done for him. Tevye still responds, "But do you love me," and eventually she responds, "I suppose I do." It is important to hear the words "I love you" from someone you love.

God wants to hear our heart of love for Him. Doing things for Him is wonderful, but also tell Him that you love Him with all your heart. Take time to spend time with Jesus. He loves to hear your love, your worship and your praise. One pattern some people use for prayer is ACTS. A is for Adoration of God; C is for Confession of sin; T is for Thanksgiving for God's blessings; and S is for Supplication — asking God for specific requests.

It is also important to pray in faith. The Bible says "Ask and it will be given to you; seek and you will find; knock and the door will be opened to you. For everyone who asks receives; he who seeks finds; and to him who knocks, the door will be opened."[15]

Yonggi Cho is the pastor of Full Gospel Central Church in Seoul, Korea. Years ago when he was starting his ministry, he was very poor and was praying to God for a chair and a bicycle. As he prayed diligently, he felt God's peace and assurance in his heart that God would indeed provide him with a chair and a bicycle. So, Yonggi began to proclaim in faith that he would get that chair and bicycle. He even told his friends it was as if he was pregnant with a chair and bicycle. Though his friends laughed at him, some time later Yonggi did receive the answer to his prayers — a chair and a bicycle. During the process of waiting on God he learned an important lesson about asking in faith.

The Bible says "Therefore I tell you, whatever you ask for in prayer, believe that you have received it, and it will be yours."[16] This doesn't mean that you automatically get everything you pray for; we need to ask God for wisdom to pray according to His will, and often we need to be patient.

And finally, pray for others. The Bible says "Therefore confess your sins to each other and pray for each other so that you may be healed. The prayer of a righteous man is powerful and effective."[17] Don't let your prayers just be for yourself, but pray for your family, for friends, for loved ones, and for the leaders of your country. Jesus Himself prayed for His disciples; He even taught us to "Love your enemies and pray for those who persecute you."[18] You can pray for others that they will come to know God and that they will have the joy of having Jesus Christ in their lives. By your very prayers, you can help bring blessing and peace to others and can help transform the world for Jesus Christ.

God gives us the tremendous privilege of spending time with Him each day. So the fifth key to Christian growth is to spend time with God.

# KEY 6

# Share Christ
# With Others

Bill Bright was founder of Campus Crusade for Christ. Bill was a businessman who gave his life to Christ and then dedicated his life to reaching others. On a personal basis, he was probably best known for sharing Christ with people wherever he would go. On one occasion, Bill was on a trip to New York City, to visit a donor who had pledged a significant amount of money. The plane was running late and the person traveling with Bill was in a hurry so that they both could meet the wealthy gentleman. When they got to New York, Bill's traveling companion was hurrying for a taxi and suddenly realized that Bill was not there to take the taxi with him. Looking around, he saw Bill sharing Christ with two porters who helped people with their luggage. Going back to try and hurry Bill, he was nicely informed by Bill that he was sharing

Christ with these two porters, and the rich gentleman would have to wait. Bill had the right priorities.

Bill would sometimes ask people, "What is the greatest thing that happened to you?" If you are a Christian, you would probably say "accepting Jesus Christ as Savior is the greatest thing that happened to me."

Jesus said the two greatest commandments were "Love the Lord your God with all your heart and with all your soul and with all your mind and with all your strength. The second is this: 'Love your neighbor as yourself.'"[1] He said all the law depended on these two commandments. When we look at how we should live our lives with those around us, our greatest commandment is to love our neighbor as ourselves. What greater way can we love them than by sharing Christ with them?

In the mid-1800's in Chicago, a young shoe salesman named Dwight Moody had a large Sunday school full of children and teenagers. One day one of the teachers in his Sunday school came to Dwight saying that he had been diagnosed with a fatal illness, and would have to leave Chicago to try to recover his health. In great distress, the school teacher said that his entire Sunday school class of teenage girls were not Christians, and he asked Dwight to accompany him to visit each of those girls.

Over the next few days, they rode by horse and buggy to visit each one of those high school girls. The dying teacher poured out his heart to each girl, presenting clearly the gospel of Christ, and asked if she would receive Christ. By the time the teacher got on the train to leave, every single one of the girls in his class had accepted Jesus Christ as their Savior.

Jesus said to His disciples, "Go into all the world and preach the good news to all creation."[2] As a Christian, the greatest thing that you can do for someone else is to help lead them to Jesus Christ. Our life on earth is so short. As Christians, we have the gift of eternal life; we have the gift of forgiveness of sins here on this earth and of eternal life in heaven forever with Jesus. We also know that God "wants all men to be saved and to come to a knowledge of the truth."[3]

How can we help others to come to know Jesus Christ? It may be tempting to say that is the job of the church, or a pastor or a professional evangelist, but God may want to use you. Every day there may be people that God gives us opportunities to talk to about Jesus, and God has given us the power of the Holy Spirit to be His witnesses. Jesus said "You will receive power when the Holy Spirit comes on you; and you will be My witnesses in Jerusalem, and in all Judea and Samaria, and to the ends of the earth."[4] Many non-Christians will never go to a church or go to hear Billy Graham, but they will listen to someone who they know and trust. You can ask God to give you His love and strength so you can help others come to know Jesus Christ.

There are many ways you can help others come to know Christ. You can pray for people you know, or pray for people around the world. You can send evangelistic emails to people. You can contribute money to your church and other good Christian organizations that are helping to reach people for Jesus Christ.

Perhaps most importantly, you can be used by God to reach people in your own sphere of influence. The Bible even calls us ambassadors — "We are therefore Christ's ambassadors, as though God were making His appeal through us. We implore you on Christ's behalf: Be reconciled to God."[5] One day I was at work and a co-worker came in and asked what I was doing that weekend. It was Easter weekend, and so without much thought I said "I'm going to church and praise the Lord." This started a conversation, and we ended up going to lunch at a Mexican restaurant the next week. We talked over lunch; I read through a short evangelistic booklet "The Four Spiritual Laws" with him and he prayed to receive Christ.

How do we share Christ? There are many ways to do this. Bill Bright wrote "The Four Spiritual Laws" which has been used by millions of people to help share their faith with others. The booklet gives a short, clear presentation of the gospel; asks people if they would like to pray to receive Christ; then gives them a sample prayer which they can pray to invite Christ into their life. It is designed in such a way that you could sit down and read this to someone, thus making it very simple to present the gospel. The booklet is available from Campus Crusade for Christ. You can also send someone a link to an evangelistic website such as www.GodLovesTheWorld.com to share Christ with friends or people that you know.

It is important to pray for those whom you want to tell about Jesus. Paul said "I urge, then, first of all, that requests, prayers, intercession and thanksgiving be made for everyone."[6] Charles Finney was an evangelist in New York State in the 1800's. He would travel from town to town presenting the gospel and many people prayed to receive Christ under his ministry. One of the keys to the success of his ministry was that before he would go to a town, a friend of his called Brother Nash would often go to that town and spend days in prayer, praying for the people in that town to come to know Jesus Christ. When Finney would show up, he might be told that there was a man crying out and spending all of his time in his room, groaning before God. Finney knew that Brother Nash was there praying for him. You may not have a Brother Nash who goes before you, but you can take time and pray yourself that God would touch the hearts of your family members, friends and people you come in contact with.

Ben, a successful real estate developer whose life was transformed by Christ, has become a lifelong witness for Jesus Christ. A short while ago Ben was on a trip with another businessman. The businessman, a young man in his thirties, was the successful head of a large business. This businessman was not married, had many girlfriends and was living a very luxurious life.

After a full day together, the businessman turned to Ben and asked him why Ben had married his wife. In this day and age, people can just live together without being married. Ben responded with the idea that he got married because he wanted to do what was right before God. This started a long conversation, and by the time the conversation was over, the young businessman had prayed and asked Jesus Christ into his life. He left Ben saying it was the best day of his life.

We should be ready to talk to people about Jesus Christ. Paul in his letter to Timothy in the Bible said "Always be prepared to give an answer to everyone who asks you to give the reason for the hope that you have."[7] There are Christian groups such as Campus Crusade for Christ, Evangelism Explosion, and the Contagious Christian course that can help you be prepared to witness for Jesus Christ. I took a course like this once in New York City. After a couple of hours of classroom training, we were sent out into the streets of New York with copies of the Four Spiritual Laws to talk to people about Jesus Christ. I think all of us were quite scared and nervous, and most of us were probably sure that we would experience great rejection. You can imagine my surprise when, in New York's Central Park, someone prayed with me to receive Jesus Christ.

Bill Bright once found a survey which said that most people did not even know how to become a Christian. He wept when he read this and said "They just don't know how." Jesus said to His disciples "All authority in heaven and on earth has been given to Me. Therefore go and make disciples of all nations, baptizing them in the name of the Father and of the Son and of the Holy Spirit, and teaching them to obey everything I have commanded you. And surely I am with you always, to the very end of the age."[8]

Even though you may be scared and very aware of your own inadequacies, Jesus Christ is with you and the Holy Spirit can work through you to share the gospel of Jesus Christ. Bill Bright would say "Successful witnessing is sharing Christ in the power of the Holy Spirit and leaving the results to God." You may or may not see people pray to receive Christ, but you can have the joy of sharing Christ in the power of the Holy Spirit and knowing that you may help someone spend eternity with Jesus.

Here are two practical steps to help you in witnessing. First, learn to share "God's story" — a gospel presentation that is clear and understandable. Second, learn to tell "your story" — how God has changed your life. Remember, our role is to point people to Christ, our Savior. "And how can they believe in the One of Whom they have not heard? And how can they hear without someone preaching to them?"[9] We are a witness of what He has done in our lives. The job of the Holy Spirit is to convict people's hearts and draw them to Jesus. Our role is to be a messenger of the good news.

If someone you know does pray to receive Jesus Christ, they are now like a newborn baby spiritually. You can have the privilege of helping that new baby grow. When I became a Christian many years ago, there was a man named Michael who helped me learn to study the Bible and provided great Christian teaching. The next year, he and his family gave me a place to live as I began to grow in my Christian life. You can help new Christians get connected to a church and get involved in a Bible study, and can help teach them principles of prayer and growth as a Christian.

While witnessing to someone is the greatest thing you can do for them spiritually, there are many other ways to show God's love to others. You can help feed the poor; care for the sick; visit those in prison; or show kindness to someone who is downhearted.

Sometimes it's just showing simple kindness to a stranger in need. A minister named Chip tells the story of a large gathering of students who went to hear a noted Bible teacher. When they all left the building and drove away, it was pouring rain. On the side of the road, as the students drove by, there was a broken down car with a man trying to fix the engine. Sadly, many other cars had already passed this man by, but Chip's friend pulled over the car to stop and help. There in the pouring rain, Chip's friend spent an hour and a half helping the man to fix his car and finally took him to a gas station to help. This is one example of practical Christian love. Jesus said "Love your neighbor as yourself."[10] You can look for daily opportunities to show Christ's love to others.

Jesus sent His disciples into the world to change the world — to give people the life changing message of hope in Jesus Christ. You and I, as followers of Christ, have the same privilege. You can ask God to give you a vision for changing the world for Jesus Christ. The evangelist Dwight Moody was inspired when he heard someone say that God was waiting to see what could be done with someone who was totally yielded to Him. Dwight, who was a shoe salesman at the time, realized that the man wasn't referring to someone great or talented or perfect; he just said "yielded." Dwight said "I want to be that man," and God used him greatly.

What is God calling you to do? Maybe you can pray for a country somewhere in the world and God will greatly use your prayers. God may call you to reach out to people yourself in some way. You can give financially to Christian organizations that are preaching the gospel around the world; your contribution can help lead someone to Christ. You could also help in the work of your church or another Christian organization. Ask God to give you a vision so that someday in heaven, you'll be able to meet people that God has used you to bring to Jesus Christ.

Bill Bright once wrote a book entitled "Come Help Change the World." There are many different ways we can reach people for Christ. We can do so by one on one witnessing, by praying for others, by contributing financially, by sending evangelistic e-mails, or by going to another part of the world. The Bible says "How beautiful are the feet of those who bring good news."[11] You can have the joy and privilege of helping to reach the world for Jesus Christ. So the sixth key to Christian growth is to share Christ with others.

May God bless you by His Holy Spirit as you apply these 6 keys in your life.

# Scripture References

**KEY 1 — BE SURE YOU ARE A CHRISTIAN**
[1] John 1:12
[2] John 3:16
[3] Romans 10:9
[4] Romans 10:9
[5] 1 John 5:11
[6] Genesis 1:1
[7] 1 John 4:16
[8] Isaiah 53:5, 6
[9] John 6:28, 29
[10] Romans 3:23
[11] Romans 3:10
[12] John 10:10
[13] Romans 6:23
[14] Romans 5:8
[15] Romans 6:23
[16] John 1:12
[17] 1 John 5:11, 12
[18] 1 John 1:9

## KEY 2 — BE FILLED WITH THE HOLY SPIRIT
[1] Acts 1:8
[2] John 3: 2–8
[3] Acts 1:4, 5
[4] Acts 2:4
[5] Ephesians 5:18
[6] Luke 11:13
[7] Colossians 1:27
[8] John 15:5
[9] Galatians 5:16
[10] Galatians 5:22, 23
[11] John 15:26

## KEY 3 — LEARN GOD'S WORD
[1] Psalm 119:105
[2] Matthew 4:4
[3] Ephesians 6:10, 11, 17
[4] 2 Timothy 3:16, 17
[5] Proverbs 11:2
[6] 2 Timothy 3:17
[7] Psalm 150:6
[8] Psalm 145:2
[9] Psalm 95:2
[10] Psalm 119:89
[11] Psalm 119:97

[12] Hebrews 4:12
[13] Psalm 119:11
[14] Psalm 119:9
[15] Psalm 119:42

## KEY 4 — BE INVOLVED IN CHURCH
[1] Hebrews 10:25
[2] Acts 2:42, 44, 46–47
[3] Colossians 1:18
[4] Ephesians 1:22, 23
[5] Matthew 18:20
[6] Matthew 7:12
[7] Psalm 66:8
[8] Acts 12:5
[9] Matthew 18:19
[10] Acts 2:46
[11] Proverbs 27:17
[12] James 1:5

## KEY 5 — SPEND TIME WITH GOD
[1] Matthew 18:3
[2] Hebrews 13:5
[3] Matthew 28:20
[4] Matthew 6:9
[5] Matthew 6:10
[6] Matthew 6:11

[7] Matthew 6:12
[8] Matthew 6:13
[9] Matthew 6:13
[10] Luke 18:1
[11] Psalm 5:3
[12] Psalm 100:4
[13] Mark 12:30, 31
[14] Psalm 150:2
[15] Matthew 7:7, 8
[16] Mark 11:24
[17] James 5:16
[18] Matthew 5:44

## KEY 6 — SHARE CHRIST WITH OTHERS
[1] Mark 12:30, 31
[2] Mark 16:15
[3] 1 Timothy 2:4
[4] Acts 1:8
[5] 2 Corinthians 5:20
[6] 1 Timothy 2:1
[7] 1 Peter 3:15
[8] Matthew 28:18–20
[9] Romans 10:14
[10] Mark 12:31
[11] Romans 10:15